Pu by
Tutor Master Services

With grateful thanks to Christine for helping to prepare this book

David Malindine

Tutor Master Services
61 Ashness Gardens
Greenford
Middlesex
UB6 0RW

Email: david@tutormaster-services.co.uk

Contents

How to use this book

These story plans are designed to help students to write their own stories. The plans encourage them to think about their own experiences as topics for their own stories.

Students should read through the story plans and then think about how they can tell their story by including their personal experiences into the framework that is provided. Asking adults to help them remember details is useful but the students should be encouraged to write independently.

Tutor Master suggests that stories should be written as a first draft, which can then be corrected. After this a final (best) copy can be produced which the writer can be proud of.

Parts of Speech – The jobs that words do in sentences

When you are writing your stories don't forget that different words have different jobs to do. Here are some of the main types of words and their jobs.

- **Nouns** – these are *naming* words. **Common nouns** are the names of ordinary things, e.g. book, pen, ruler. **Proper nouns** are the names of important things, people and places; they begin with capital letters, e.g. Christmas, John, London.

- **Adjectives** – these are *describing* words; they describe nouns, e.g. large, beautiful, wicked.

- **Verbs** – these are *doing* words or *action* words, e.g. dancing, running, jumping. They are also *being* words, e.g. is, was, were, am, are.

- **Adverbs** – these help to describe verbs, they tell how, when and where an action takes place. Adverbs often end in 'ly', e.g. quickly, slowly.

- **Conjunctions (Connectives)** – these are *joining* words, which help to put words and sentences together. You can use them in your stories to make your sentences longer, e.g. and, so, but, because.

- **Pronouns** – these words can be used to replace nouns and to save you repeating yourself, e.g. she, he, we, they.

- **Prepositions** – these words connect two nouns in a sentence and tell you the position of one thing in relation to another, e.g. on, in, under.

- **Similes** – these are comparisons which use the words 'like' and 'as'. You can use similes to make your writing more interesting and exciting, e.g. Don drove *like a maniac*, Mary was *as good as gold*, the moon was *like a lump of yellow cheese*.

- **Metaphors** – these are phrases or sentences which compare two things by saying that something *is* something else, e.g. the moon *is a big lump of yellow cheese*, she *is full of beans*, he *is a real live wire*. (A metaphor is different from a simile because you do not use 'like' or 'as').

Some feelings you can include in your stories

You can use these examples of feelings in your stories. Check their meanings in a dictionary to make sure you are using them correctly. Use a thesaurus to add new examples to your own feelings bank.

Good feelings

cheerful	merry
joyful	jolly
delighted	light hearted
pleased	contented
satisfied	thrilled
elated	overjoyed
glad	grateful
happy	thankful
amused	uplifted
inspired	motivated
encouraged	excited
carefree	excellent
superb	outstanding
magnificent	exceptional
marvellous	wonderful
fantastic	terrific
brilliant	eager
determined	enthusiastic
amazed	stunning
enjoy	splendid

Bad feelings

sorrowful — sad
unhappy — miserable
depressed — downcast
despondent — wretched
glum — gloomy
dismal — tragic
awful — woeful
discouraged — dejected
worried — troubled
dreary — anxious
useless — pathetic
grim — grumpy
grouchy — cross
terrible — frightful
dreadful — afraid
fearful — ghastly
nasty — horrible
vile — revolting
nervous — horrified
frightened — panicky

The ingredients for a good story

When you are writing a story you should remember these things:-

1. Try to write a story that comes from your own experience. You have some great stories of your own to tell so now is your chance to tell them.

2. Do your best to make your story sound true, even if it isn't.

3. Make sure your story has a beginning, a middle and an end.

4. Make sure you know how your story will end before you begin.

5. Be careful to punctuate your work carefully, using capital letters, full stops, commas, question marks, exclamation marks and apostrophes.

6. Write good descriptions using adjectives, adverbs and similes.

7. Start a new paragraph each time you change the topic you are writing about.

8. Make sure you describe your feelings or the feelings of the characters you are writing about.

9. Include some direct speech correctly punctuated, using the rules for punctuating direct speech:

   a) Always begin speech with a capital letter, e.g.
   "I've got too much homework today."

b) Enclose the actual words that are spoken with speech marks, e.g.

Geoff said, "I've got too much homework today."

c) Separate the words that are actually spoken from the other words with a comma, e.g.

Geoff said, "I've got too much homework today."

d) Make sure question marks and exclamation marks are enclosed within the speech marks, e.g.

"Why are you always complaining about homework?" asked Anne.

e) When writing speech conversation or dialogue, make sure you write a new speaker on a new line, e.g.

"I'm not always complaining about homework," replied Geoff.

"Oh yes, you are!" shouted Anne.

10. Be careful to spell correctly especially with words you know you find difficult.

11. It's a good idea to write your stories in the *past tense* as you will find it easier to maintain this throughout the story.

MY FIRST DAY AT SCHOOL

Write about your first day at school.

It could be the very first day that you started school (if you can remember!) or it could be the first day you started at infants, primary or secondary school. If you have moved school you could write about the move from your old school to the new one.

Beginning

Start by explaining which school you are going to write about and say whether it was Nursery, Reception or which Year you were going to begin.

Did you have a uniform to wear? If so, describe what it was like.

How did you feel the night before, in the morning and on the way?

How did you get to school on that first day? Did someone go with you?

What happened when you got to school? Explain how you were put in a class and met your new teacher for the first time. Did another pupil in the class look after you? Write some speech conversation between yourself and your new teacher or a classmate.

If most people in the class were new, how did you make friends? Did you sit next to someone? Did you become friends with them?

Middle

Describe what the classroom looked like. How were the desks and chairs arranged? Describe the wall displays.

Tell about the children that you met and their names. Write about all the things you did on that first day. (If you can't remember use your imagination to make up some ideas.)

Tell about what you did at playtime. What games did you play? Who did you play with?

What happened at lunchtime? Did you have a school lunch or did you take your own food?

Describe the different kinds of work activities that you did on that first day.

End

Write about getting ready to go home. Was your mum or dad waiting? What did you say when you saw them? What did they say to you?

Tell about the particular memories that you have of that first day.

A LETTER TO A RELATIVE

As part of your English lessons you have been taught how to set out a letter correctly on a page. This letter will give you the chance to practise your letter writing skills by giving you the ideas to help you write to someone you may know but do not see as often as you would like.

Beginning

You should put your home address and the date at the top right hand side of your letter. You should then begin your letter in an informal and friendly way, e.g. 'Dear...' (followed by the person's name).

Introduce yourself, and tell them about yourself. Tell how old you are or how tall. (You decide how much personal information you need to give them depending on when you last had contact).

Middle

Tell them about how you are getting on at school, which Year you are in, which subjects you are good at and the ones you enjoy.

Give some examples of some things you have done at school and have had success with.

Tell them some things about your family and the people you live with. Mention some of the things that you enjoy doing with them.

Tell them about some of the things that you enjoy doing out of school. Do you belong to any clubs or societies to do with sport, drama, music, religion or culture?

End

To finish off, describe any places you have visited recently, or any of the things that you did during your last school holiday. Maybe thank them for any birthday or other presents they have sent you. Remember to end the letter with 'Love from' or 'From' or 'Best wishes' and add your name so they know who the letter is from.

When you have finished ask someone for an envelope and for the address of your relative (if you do not know it already), stick on the correct postage stamp, post the letter, sit back and wait for the reply!

MY DREAM HOUSE

In the story describe in detail the best house you could have. You should also describe the garden too. This is your chance to say what you would like to have if you could plan your house yourself.

Beginning

Describe the house: say how many floors there are and how many rooms are upstairs and downstairs. Say if your house would be detached, semi-detached or terraced.

Tell how many bathrooms, kitchens, bedrooms and other rooms there would be. How would the house be decorated?

Describe the size and layout of the garden: tell about what you would like to have in the garden e.g. swimming pool, tennis courts, slides and swings.

Middle

Describe in more detail the rooms that you would spend most time in.

Tell about the size, decoration and colours of your bedroom.

Maybe you would have a hobby room or a playroom. Describe the things and equipment you would have in there, e.g. T.V., computer and stereo system, a desk for doing homework and shelves for your books.

Perhaps there would be a snooker or table-tennis table for relaxation and fun. Would there be cushions on the floor or comfy chairs and a sofa to relax on?

End

Finish by thinking about all the things that are most important to you in your dream house.

Say which item or room is most important to you and how you would feel if you could have it added to the house you live in now. Perhaps you have it already, in which case tell how you couldn't bear to live without it.

MY PERFECT DAY AT THE WEEKEND

The weekends are a great time for us to rest and enjoy ourselves after a busy week. In this story you are to choose a day and describe what happens and what you do to have a great time.

If you want, you can choose a day that really happened and write about it. Another idea would be to imagine all the possible things that could happen and then make them all happen on one day.

Your story does not have to be true but it does need to sound true.

Beginning

Write about waking up and realising that it is the weekend. Maybe you go through in your mind the things you have planned.

Describe getting up and having breakfast without all the rush that normally comes on a weekday. What do you do first? Do you watch some morning TV programmes and then maybe talk to your parents about what to do? Include some speech conversation.

Maybe your parents are going out to the shops. Will you go too? Write about the arrangements that are made for the rest of the day.

Middle

Describe the things you do next. Are you at home for lunch or out for lunch? Maybe you meet your friends. Do you go to their house or do they come to you? What things do you do with them?

Perhaps you arrange to meet your friends to go into town to the shops or to the cinema. Maybe you go swimming or ice-skating. Describe the things that you enjoy doing most. Include some speech conversation.

When evening comes, you have another meal. It could be your favourite. Describe the meal.

After you've eaten, you may decide to go out, maybe with friends, parents or relatives, or you may decide to stay in and relax. Describe what you do.

End

Later on, when you are in bed, you are thinking about all the things you have enjoyed during the day. Tell the reader about the things that particularly stand out and which you have enjoyed the most.

MYSELF

In this story, try to imagine that you are describing yourself to someone who doesn't really know you. This is your chance to tell about yourself so make the most of it!

Write about all the things that you know about yourself that you would like others to know too.

Beginning

Introduce yourself. You could do this using the kind of information that appears in a passport, e.g. age, date of birth, place of birth, eye colour, hair colour and your height.

Describe your appearance, what you look like and the clothes you wear. Explain how this may change depending on whom you are with or where you are going, e.g. describe your school uniform and also what you might wear to a wedding or a party. Describe your favourite casual clothes too.

Tell the reader about your personality and character as well. Are you a cheerful, friendly, happy person or a miserable, unfriendly and unhappy person? (You may be a mixture of all of these at times!). Say where you live and what the place is like where you live. Write about your family and say a little about the people you live with.

Middle

Write about the things that you enjoy doing at home. What are your hobbies and interests? Explain why you like these things.

Describe your school and say what you like doing and what success you have had. Write about your class and your teacher. What things do you dislike at school? Who are your friends at school and at home? Write about some of the things you do with them. Write about the things you do at their houses. What things do you do when they come to your house?

What are your favourite foods and drinks? What books do you like to read and who is your favourite author?

End

Write about what you hope to do when you are older. What job would you like? Are there any things you would like to do when you are older that you can't do now?

THE GIFT

Try to base the story on an occasion when you received a gift and make the story as interesting and exciting as you can.

Make sure you use good descriptions with adjectives and adverbs. Also try to include speech conversation and make sure it is correctly punctuated.

Describe your feelings and the feelings of other characters too.

Beginning

Tell the reader about the gift. Describe carefully what it looked like. Was it wrapped up? If so, say what it looked like in its paper. Write about your feelings when you were given the gift. Did you know what it was? Could you guess?

Who gave you the gift? Why were you given it? Was it for a birthday or other special occasion? If the person who gave you the gift was actually there when you got it, include some lines of speech conversation between you and that person.

Middle

What did you do with the gift? What were your feelings about it? Did you write a letter to say thank you?

Write about some of the things you did with the gift. Are there any adventures that you can include?

End

Is your gift a really precious one? Do you think it is something that you will treasure and keep forever or did you keep it for a while and then find something new had taken its place? Where is your gift now?

THE FESTIVAL

During the year most of us celebrate festivals that are to do with our religious traditions, culture or beliefs. In this story you have the chance to write about a festival that you celebrate. Try to describe what happens from your own viewpoint.

Beginning

Name the festival you will be writing about. Explain briefly what the festival is about and why it is celebrated. When does your festival take place? Say what your feelings are as the festival draws near. Describe what preparations have to be made. Who does what in your family? Tell the reader about the different responsibilities that people have. What do you do?

Middle

On the day the festival begins write about what you will be doing from the time you get up. Describe your feelings. Are special food dishes being prepared? Is there a smell of cooking in the house? Describe the dishes that are being prepared. It may be that the giving and receiving of presents is a part of the festival. What are you hoping to receive? If this is a religious festival you may need to go to a place of worship. Write about some of the things you will do there. Describe what happens when you come home. When will you have your meal? Describe the eating of the meal. It would make your story better if you could include some direct speech, correctly punctuated, to set out some of the conversations that take place during the meal. Explain what happens after the meal. Maybe guests arrive. Are they friends or relatives or both? Describe anything else that happens that you feel needs to be told.

End

Tell how you feel when it's all over. Write about the clearing up afterwards. Do you have happy memories of the festival? Which memories stand out?

THE VISIT

This story could be about a time when you went to visit someone, maybe some friends or relatives. Perhaps the visit involved a journey by car and maybe you stayed for a few days.

Beginning

Say where you were going for the visit and who went with you.

Explain about whom you were going to see. Was this a visit that you were looking forward to? Was it going to be exciting? Would there be other children there for you to play with?

Describe about getting ready to go on the visit. Was there much packing to be done? What things did you need to remember to take?

Describe the packing up of the car. Was this easy to do or was there a fuss? You could include some speech conversation here. Did anything get forgotten?

Middle

Describe the journey. What things did you do to help pass the time? Did you have games to play or did you look out of the window or did you sleep?

What things were you looking forward to when you arrived? Write about arriving. Who was there to meet you?

Describe in order the things you did. Did you unpack? Did you have a meal, what is said? Write some speech conversation, correctly punctuated.

Write about some of the things you did on your visit. Write about them in as interesting a way as you can. You do not have to write about every little thing but focus on the things you especially enjoyed.
Remember to include your feelings and put in as many details as you can to make it interesting.

End

Describe about getting ready to come home. Write about packing up and saying goodbye.

Tell the reader about your feelings. You may have been sad to be leaving but glad to be going home to your own home.

Describe the journey home. Were you looking forward to being home? What were you looking forward to?

LOST PROPERTY

Write a story about something you lost. It can be set at home or at school and it can be a big thing or a little thing that you lost. Try to base the story on something that really happened to you but you can use your imagination to fill in any details that you cannot remember.

Make sure you describe your feelings, especially the awful feelings you had when you realised that something was missing and later on the wonderful feeling you had when you found it!

Describe too the time in between losing and finding the thing. You were probably in a real panic, wondering if you would ever see it again.

Make sure you include some speech conversation during the search and punctuate it correctly.

Beginning

Begin by saying what it was that you lost. How did you know it was lost? How do you think you lost it?

Describe how you began your search. You probably began by looking in all the usual places where you leave things or where things get lost. At first you were probably quite sure that you would find what you were looking for but as you kept looking for it you started to wonder whether it really had gone for good.

Middle

You may have decided to ask mum or dad or someone else to help you. Did they agree to help? Include some of the speech conversation that took place.

As the search continued, describe your feelings and those of the person helping. Include your speech conversation correctly punctuated.

End

Describe how you felt when after looking for ages, you felt that there was no point in going on. It seemed like your hunt had been a waste of time, when suddenly, there it is! At last you find it! Now say how you felt.

Perhaps you promised that from then on you would always be so careful with your things. What did the person say who was helping you to look?

THE DAY EVERYTHING WENT WRONG

With a title like this you will need to use your imagination and also your writing skills to make your story sound believable and realistic even if some of the things that you say did not really happen. You may have had a bad day you can write about or you may like to use this as an example on which to base your story.

Beginning

You wake up late because the alarm doesn't go off. Mum calls you (put in speech). You get up and go to the bathroom but you can't have your wash because someone is there. You go back to get dressed but you can't find your tie. You go back to the bathroom but since you have been away someone else has slipped in! (Speech in here!). Eventually you get in.

Next you go downstairs for your cereal but when you go to the fridge there is no milk so you decide to have toast instead. But the toast sticks in the toaster and burns and smoke goes everywhere (describe your feelings).

You search for your homework but you can't find it. Mum says she will give you a lift to school because you are late and it's raining but when you go out the car won't start so you have to walk to school (except you run and in the process get soaked).

Middle

When you get to school it's assembly and you have to go in late (describe your feelings). Afterwards the head teacher keeps you behind and you get told off for being late and for not having your tie!

The first lesson is English but you have forgotten your homework so you get told off.

Then comes PE but you have forgotten your kit so the teacher makes you sit out and you get a break time detention.

Soon it's lunchtime but in the rush that morning you forgot to pick up your lunch box. Your friend gives you the food she doesn't want then you have to go and do your detention. (Describe what you have to do!)

In maths that afternoon a girl talks but the teacher blames you so you get kept behind after school. (Describe how you feel).

You go home late and when you get home you find you have left your key inside. Then it starts to rain, so you get wet for the second time that day.

End

When your dad comes home he tells you off for forgetting your key and for being wet. After tea you get sent to your room where you sit and think about what a dreadful day it's been.

LOST

This story should be about a time when you felt you were lost. This may be because you could not find your way somewhere or it could be about a time when you lost some people you were supposed to be with e.g. your parents, other relations or friends.

Make sure you include some direct speech punctuated correctly and good descriptions using adjectives and adverbs.

You should aim to make your story as realistic and exciting as you can.

Beginning

Write about the time when you were lost. Say when and where this happened.

Did you lose the people you were with or were you on your own and lost your way?

Explain at what point you realised that you were lost. Describe your feelings at this time.

Middle

Write what you did next and what happened.

What did you do to try to make yourself feel better? How did you get yourself out of the position you were in? Did you ask someone to help you or did you make a 'phone call?

Explain how things managed to get better and how your problems were sorted out. Did you manage to find where you wanted to go or did you find your friends or family?

Describe your feelings when you were found. What were the reactions of others? (Include some speech conversation that took place between the people who were involved in the search.)

End

What lessons did you learn from getting lost?

How do you do things differently now to try to prevent yourself getting lost?

THE VISITORS

Write a story about what happened when you had visitors come to stay at your house.

Beginning

Say who came to stay. It may just have been one person; perhaps a relative or family friend, or maybe it was your auntie and uncle plus their children, your cousins.

Describe the people, their ages, characters and personalities. Say what it was like when you met them and say where the meeting first took place. For example, it may have been at the airport when you went to pick them up. (Include the speech conversation that may have taken place.)

Describe your feelings and those of others who were there. Did the visitors bring you presents? If so, say what they were. (Write the speech conversation that took place when the presents were given and received.)

Middle

Describe some of the things you did with the visitors while they were with you.

If you went out on visits with them, describe the places you went to. Maybe you went out to restaurants to eat with them so write about where you went and what you ate. Perhaps you had some nice meals at home so describe them, say who cooked and what you did to help. (Include some direct speech of the conversations you had with the visitors.)

End

Explain how their visit ended. Were people in your family happy or sad to see the visitors leave?

Say what was the best and what was the worst bit about having the visitors to stay.

THE MAGIC CARPET

Write a story about a magic carpet. As you probably know magic carpets have amazing powers that make you fly whenever you sit on them and say the magic words.

Beginning

Write about how you discover the magic carpet. Maybe your parents buy it at a sale or in a second hand shop.

Say how you find out that the carpet has magical powers. Perhaps the carpet can speak. What would it say to you and what would you say?

Describe what the carpet looks like, its colour and pattern.

Middle

Write about the magical powers that the carpet has. Describe your feelings when it starts to do magical things. Can you control the carpet? Are you its master? Will it do as it's told?

Describe the adventures you have while flying on the carpet. Describe where you go and what you see and do. Do your parents know that you can fly to anywhere in the world that you want?

Tell of the good things you do to make the world a better, safer place. Perhaps you receive a medal from the Queen for the good works that you do.

Perhaps you and your family get great riches from being the owners of the magic carpet.

End

Write about what happens in the end. Maybe you use up the magic carpet's amazing powers. Perhaps the magic carpet just becomes an ordinary carpet again. Then again perhaps its powers are being stored for some future event. You decide!

MY FIRST BEST FRIEND

Write a story about the first best friend you ever had. If you can't remember your very first best friend, write about a friend that you have known for a long time and if possible a friend that you still have.

Beginning

Say when you met this person who was to become your best friend. Describe where you met them and how the first meeting came about. What were you doing at the time? When you first met tell what you said to each other.

Write the conversation as well as you can remember. (Don't forget to punctuate the direct speech properly, using speech marks and commas and remember to begin a new line for each new speaker).

Middle

Describe the appearance, character and personality of the person in as much detail as you can. If you met your friend at school say what sorts of things you did together.

Explain as carefully as you can what it was that especially made you want to be friends with this person, more than anyone else.

Write about some of the things you have done with this special friend that have helped your friendship to grow stronger. You may have had some adventures, which you could write about.

End

Do you think that you will always be friends with this person?

Try and say what you think are the good qualities that are needed to help a friendship to stay strong. Do you think your friendship has these qualities?

THE MAGIC RING

Write a story about a magic ring.

The story should be about a child that finds a ring. This ring turns out to have magical powers and the child has all kinds of amazing adventures. You could be in the story or it could be about another child who you could make up. You must write about what happens.

Beginning

Describe how the child finds the ring and say where they find it. Explain how the child finds out that the ring is a magic ring. (Make sure you include the names of the main characters and put in some direct speech if you can, properly punctuated).

Middle

Write about the adventures that the child has. Does the ring grant wishes? Can it make you fly? Does a genie come when you rub the magic ring? Maybe the ring can make you go back in time or maybe even into the future. Perhaps, the ring is able to transport you to countries far away. Which countries would you like to visit? What happens when you get there? What do you see? What do you do? You may even make some new friends.

End

Explain what happens at the end of your story. Does the magic ring use up all its powers? Maybe the ring gets lost again. You decide and write the best ending you can think of.

THE KEY STORY

Everybody has a story to tell about the time when they were involved with keys! It could be the time when you lost some keys or it may be the time when you, or someone you knew, left the keys in the house and went out and shut the door, locking everyone out. Or it could be the time that your mum or dad locked the keys inside the car and no one could get in. Maybe the garage man had to come to open up your car.

In this story you should tell about what happened.

Beginning

Give the background to the story. Explain what the 'key' story is to be about. Were the keys lost or locked in somewhere, i.e. what were the keys or key for? Describe where the incident happened. Who was involved?

Describe the scene. Write some direct speech to show what people were saying.

Describe as carefully as you can what people's feelings were at the time. Were they panicking or did they think it was funny?

Middle

Describe what happened next. What was done to try to put things right and make things better?

Describe what actions were taken and say who took them. If you were involved, include what you did and what your feelings were.

Did the situation improve? (Make sure you continue to write some conversations between the people involved).

End

Tell what happened in the end. What was the final outcome of the 'key' story?

After it was all over describe the feelings of those people who had been involved. Were they relieved, cross or tired? What did people say and do? What lessons do you think could be learned from this experience?

TEAMWORK

Most people have, at some time or another, been part of a team. Maybe for you it was in a sports team. Perhaps this was at school representing your House, Class or Form, or maybe even the school. Maybe the team you were in was not a sport one but a quiz team, a chess team or even something like a team for a maths challenge. It could be that the team you were a part of met outside of school, perhaps a sports team such as cricket, rugby, swimming or tennis that you did as a hobby.   Perhaps you were in a dance class, a choir or an orchestra where you had to work together.

In this story you will be writing about what it is like to be a part of a team.

Beginning

Write about the team you were in. You may want to write a description of the team and tell about how long you have been involved and what part you play in the team.

Write something too about some of the other characters that are in the team. Include what you think makes your team do its best. Say what you think makes good teamwork.

Middle

Write about a particular time when your team did well and achieved success. Maybe this was a time when your team did much better than everyone expected. Perhaps the whole team worked really well together and tried really hard so that you achieved a great result.

Write about what you did to help the team and what some other members of the team did that helped the team succeed.

Describe your feelings and those of some other characters' during your team's performance.

End

At the end write about how you felt. What did other people say about your performance and those of your teammates after the event? Write some speech conversation between the team members and between some spectators who saw the performance.

Did you win a prize or an award for what you had done? Perhaps there was a ceremony where you were given the award. When you think back, say what it was that gave you the best feeling of teamwork.

THE TIME I ACHIEVED AN AWARD

Most of you, at sometime, will have received an award for achieving something. This may be something you have achieved at school or out of school. Perhaps in school you have worked hard at a project or you have been successful in a competition and this has led to you receiving a prize or an award. Maybe you have had success out of school perhaps in a club, music or dance festival, society, team or organisation.

In this story you should describe what you were awarded and how you went about achieving it.

Beginning

Begin by describing what it was that you were working hard to achieve. Explain the background to the challenge and in detail say what you had to do.

Say also whether this was a team effort or something you did on your own.

Write about your feelings and your hopes and fears at this time.

Middle

Describe how the competition progressed and who was judging it. Describe carefully what happened. (Make sure you describe your feelings and include direct speech, correctly punctuated).

Explain what challenges you faced and say how you reacted to them. What did other people say to you about how you were doing? Were there any times when you thought you would fail? Who encouraged you to keep going? Say when it was that you knew you had been successful. Describe your feelings at this time.

Go on to write about the actual presentation of the award. Who presented it to you? Where did the presentation take place? What were you given as the award?

End

After describing the presentation of the award, write about what happened next. What did people say to you? What have you done with the award? Do you treasure it? Did you have to pass it back a year later? Was it something which could be engraved with your name?

Say what you have learned as a result of gaining the award.

THE BIRTHDAY PARTY

Most of us have had a birthday party or have been to someone else's party. In this story you should write about a birthday party you have had or one you have been to. It maybe that the party was held at someone's house, or maybe it was held somewhere different like at a burger restaurant, a leisure centre, a bowling alley or an ice rink.

In this story you should write all about the party, in as exciting a way as you can.

Beginning

Whose birthday were you celebrating? Was the party held at a house or somewhere else?

Describe the preparations that were made. Write about how the party was organised and who sent out the invitations. Maybe decorations had to be put up. Who decided what the food would be? Where did people have to meet?

Middle

Describe your feelings on the day of the party. Describe what you wore for the occasion. Perhaps you took a present. Describe what it was.

If it was your party, say how you felt as the guests arrived. Did they bring presents? Describe what you got.

Now write about how the party went. Describe carefully what happened. Say if there were any moments that stand out when things happened that were really good, really funny or really disastrous! (Make sure you include some direct speech, correctly punctuated, as you set out some of the conversations).

Describe the birthday cake, the food and the drinks that you had.

Write about when the party was finishing. Were there party bags to take home? Did everyone leave together or did some of the best friends stay on longer?

End

When the party was all over and everyone had gone, say how you felt. What were the best and worst bits of the day?

Is there another birthday or similar celebration that you are looking forward to next?

MY FIRST FAVOURITE TOY

Think back to the first toy you had which you couldn't put down.

Beginning

Tell the reader what your first favourite toy was. Describe what it looked like.

Say where you got it. Was it a present from someone? If it was a present write some speech conversation between you and the person who gave the toy.

Explain why you especially liked it.

Middle

Explain the sorts of things that you did with the toy.

Describe some of the memories that you have of it. Did you have fun? Tell about some adventures that you had.

Did you ever lose the toy? Describe what happened and the feelings you had.

What games did you play with the toy?

End

Have you still got the toy? Do you ever use it now? Is it stored away, and if it is, do you ever miss it?

What do you play with now that has replaced it?